FAITH

TO

LIVE

BY

With thanks to Debbie Palaniappan and Kate Efomi for their patience and proofreading and to David McNeill from Revo Creative for cover design and typesetting.

Published in the United Kingdom by:
Destiny Leadership Resources
Destiny Ministries
70 Cathedral Street
Glasgow, G4 0RD

Telephone: 0141 616 6777
Email: dlr@destiny-church.com
Website: www.destinyleadershipresources.com
Twitter: @DLR3000
Follow Sue on Twitter at @OwenSue

Printed by Bell and Bain Ltd, Glasgow

FAITH
TO
LIVE
BY

SUE OWEN

Destiny
Leadership Resources

FAITH TO LIVE BY WORKBOOK

The Bible is the most creative, life-enhancing book you will ever find and it will share your journey all the way. A fresh word sought out often will keep you and help you to be one step ahead. This is your journey of faith and you may be excited or seriously desperate right now. Thank you for choosing this workbook and for inviting me—through it—into your life today! I have been praying that as you work through the pages of this book it will help you! You will need to be honest, committed and focussed but by the power of the Holy Spirit change will come and new ground will be taken.

Your prayer and honesty will take you through many moments. Some will be restful, some will be challenging, with (I'm believing) many high points along the way. One thing is for sure: tomorrow is on its way and you have a destiny that God has designed for you! Every new day of the season that you are in is precious and full of purpose. Don't miss the value of each day through frustration or impatience. Work with God every step of the way. He has promised that He will not leave you!

JOSHUA 1:9

Be strong, vigorous, and very courageous. Be not afraid, neither be dismayed, for the Lord your God is with you wherever you go.

I have two dreams concerning this book. The first is that you reach your destiny with a great cry of victory, and with this deep and earnest desire I will keep you in my prayers. The second is that possibly one day and in God's timing you may share your story. That your testimony and what you have learned will encourage others who are also searching for a breakthrough by faith.

God bless you! May He have His way, be lifted up and receive all the praise! God keep you! As you aim to grow your faith, know that He is on your side. May you see the answer you desire and above all the answer He always promised.

A note of advice as you begin.

With your notebook or journal ready, please take time to read and pray about your answers before you write. Sometimes you can react in a hurry and then you may feel trapped by the first—and possibly emotional— response that you recorded in ink. Never do that and just in case, why not record with a soft pencil so that you can rewrite your story as the word does its work, your faith grows and your experience comes into line with what God originally designed you for.

See the detail in Psalm 139 and the delight He has in you!

O Lord, you have searched me [thoroughly] and have known me. You know my down sitting and my uprising; You understand my thought afar off. You sift and search out my path and my lying down, and You are acquainted with all my ways.

For there is not a word in my tongue [still unuttered], but, behold, O Lord, You know it altogether.

You have beset me and shut me in—behind and before, and You have laid Your hand upon me. Your [infinite] knowledge is too wonderful for me; it is high above me, I cannot reach it. Where could I go from Your Spirit?

Or where could I flee from Your presence? If I ascend up into heaven, You are there; if I

*make my bed in Sheol (the place of the dead),
behold, You are there. If I take the wings of
the morning or dwell in the uttermost parts of
the sea, Even there shall Your hand lead me,
and Your right hand shall hold me.*

*If I say, Surely the darkness shall cover me
and the night shall be [the only] light about
me, Even the darkness hides nothing from
You, but the night shines as the day; the
darkness and the light are both alike to You.*

*For You did form my inward parts; You did
knit me together in my mother's womb. I will
confess and praise You for You are fearful and
wonderful and for the awful wonder of my
birth!*

*Wonderful are Your works, and that my
inner self knows right well. My frame was not
hidden from You when I was being formed in
secret [and] intricately and curiously wrought
[as if embroidered with various colours] in
the depths of the earth [a region of darkness
and mystery].*

*Your eyes saw my unformed substance, and
in Your book all the days [of my life] were*

written before ever they took shape, when as yet there was none of them. How precious and weighty also are Your thoughts to me, O God! How vast is the sum of them! If I could count them, they would be more in number than the sand. When I awoke, [could I count to the end] I would still be with You.

If You would [only] slay the wicked, O God, and the men of blood depart from me–Who speak against You wickedly, Your enemies who take Your name in vain!

Do I not hate them, O Lord, who hate You?

And am I not grieved and do I not loathe those who rise up against You? I hate them with perfect hatred; they have become my enemies. Search me [thoroughly], O God, and know my heart! Try me and know my thoughts!

And see if there is any wicked or hurtful way in me, and lead me in the way everlasting.

God knew all of your days before there was yet one of them v16–18. He knew you would be looking at life and searching for fresh faith in this season!

1

At the heart of it all everyone wants to please God and this is really affected by how we see Him, not by what we do for Him. Even before we bring our concerns we must confidently remember that God wants to answer us and He's ready and waiting. Pleasing God is about having faith in Him and trusting that He is able. It is not about our activity, emotion, energy or effort.

HEBREWS 11:6

But without faith it is impossible to please and be satisfactory to Him. For whoever would come near to God must [necessarily] believe that God exists and that He is the rewarder of those who earnestly and diligently seek Him [out].

QUESTION

Write here and read out loud to yourself how this verse has challenged or re-established your approach to God as you spend time with Him today. How does this verse shape and help to define your image of Him?

NOTES

NOTES

2

We believe that to each and every person a measure of faith is given. Faith has been given to us. We are not victims of negative thinking. We have to choose each day to not give way to any wrong thoughts that would like to overwhelm us.

ROMANS 12:3

For by the grace (unmerited favour of God) given to me I warn everyone among you not to estimate and think of himself more highly than he ought [not to have an exaggerated opinion of his own importance], but to rate his ability with sober judgement, each according to the degree of faith apportioned by God to him.

QUESTION

In the light of this scripture how do you respond to cultural or family traits that would contradict or undermine this statement? Is there anything you should address right now by repenting, changing your mind and turning away from it today?

NOTES

NOTES

3

As we begin the journey we discover that having the right attitude is very important. God will resist us if we're proud therefore we must remember that the gift is given. We are invited to bring our request before Him confidently but with respect and honour toward His word.

HABAKKUK 2:4 NKJV

Behold the proud, his soul is not upright in him: but the just shall live by his faith.

EXERCISE

Write down what you think pride and arrogance look and sound like from your experience. Where is their root to be found? Could it be fear or self- sufficiency? Explain how they can be repented of and taken out of your life.

NOTES

NOTES

4

Choosing God's wise words is like placing armour in between the problem and the breakthrough. Defining then protecting our preferred answer becomes the issue. We must use our faith as a shield to protect ourselves and others. We deliberately position our faith to protect us from the discouraging and distracting darts of the enemy.

EPHESIANS 6:16

Lift up over all the [covering] shield of saving faith, upon which you can quench all the flaming missiles of the wicked [one].

QUESTION

How did discouragement come to you or those you know? Describe the vehicle and route of the attack. Think prayerfully about it for a while. Was it by words spoken over you, thoughts that took root and overwhelmed you or previous experiences?

Do not write your answers down or speak them out in any detail or content, for as from today you do not need to give them any more thought, breathing space or airtime.

Instead please pray this prayer with me...

Father God I thank You that You know me and You are acquainted with all my ways, and You love me through Jesus your Son.

I acknowledge these negative thoughts, these words and experiences.

I do not believe that they were sent by You or that they are a part of Your divine plan for my life.

I cut them off now in the name of The Lord, and I break their power in Jesus name.

In faith I plead the blood of Jesus in the name of Jesus over these foul and negative things.

I pray grace, grace, grace over my life and expect only good to come and full of blessing, for Your glory.

Thank you that Jesus came to give me abundant life and I receive it now in His name.

Amen

NOTES

NOTES

5

The Lord does not want us to be naively duped by every or any tactic of the enemy. He wants us to be ahead of the game, praying with authority and His insight over our decisions.

PSALM 89:22

The enemy shall not exact from him or do him violence or outwit him, nor shall the wicked afflict and humble him.

TASK

Every time you pray things through today, ask The Lord to give you His wisdom, insight and understanding. Once you've heard, ask for the ability to put into action what He has said.

NOTES

NOTES

6

We know that the enemy is real, always has bad intentions and only ever comes along in order to kill, thieve or destroy. He also tries to put a full stop where God would place a comma. Although he is full of mischief, the truth is our life is out of bounds for him.

JOHN 10:10 NKJV

The thief does not come EXCEPT to steal, and to kill, and to destroy. I have come that they may have life, and that they may have it more abundantly.

STUDY

How did your understanding of your
position change when you accepted
that Jesus died and rose again for you?
Knowing, accepting and confessing these
truths is essential. Search out, think on and
write down scriptures that describe how
your position shifted commercially, legally,
spiritually, royally and physically. Scriptures
with 'in Christ' will help you here and they
are very exciting!

NOTES

NOTES

7

Just as the enemy would only come along to try and produce disaster, the word of God is always sent to the door of our heart and mind with powerful blessing and good intent!

ISAIAH 55:10-11

For as the rain and snow come down from the heavens, and return not there again, but water the earth and make it bring forth and sprout, that it may give seed to the sower and bread to the eater, So shall My word be that goes forth out of My mouth: it shall not return to Me void [without producing any effect, useless], but it shall accomplish that which I please and purpose, and it shall prosper in the thing for which I sent it.

TASK

Write out these verses in full with the reference. Take time to think on these words at four or five points today. Choose one word that is impacting you, dwell on it specifically and note how it is affecting you today.

Encourage someone by emailing this scripture to a friend!

NOTES

NOTES

8

We need order when seeking for and serving God. The universe is full of rhythm and pattern. It's no different in our spiritual life and we must do things God's way as submission comes before authority. We can resist the enemy because in our lives we've first set the balance of power right.

JAMES 4:7

So be subject to God. Resist the devil (stand firm against him) and he will flee from you.

TASK

List three things that you have brought into line with this biblical principle, pray into them and choose to be delighted that God takes you at your word.

NOTES

NOTES

9

The will of God is the key for us as it brings with it outrageous and acceptable boldness. We place our confidence in His will and value what He values. We search to find out what scriptural promise fits our situation and begin to pray confidently.

1 JOHN 5:14-15 NKJV

Now this is the confidence that we have in Him, that if we ask anything according to His will He hears us. And if we know that He hears us, whatever we ask, we know that we have the petitions that we have asked of Him.

Read it again here in the Amplified Bible

1 John 5:14-15 And this is the confidence (the assurance, the privilege of boldness) which we have in Him: [we are sure] that if we ask anything (make any request) according to His will (in agreement with His own plan), He listens to and hears us.

And if (since) we [positively] know that He listens to us in whatever we ask, we also know [with settled and absolute knowledge] that we have [granted us as our present possessions] the requests made of Him.

TASK

Write these verses out on a piece of card and put them where you will see them every day. Read them out loud to yourself each day for a month. Take note of how your prayer vocabulary changes by the end of the first week.

NOTES

NOTES

10

Here we acknowledge that the word of God has plenty to say to us and it is extremely important in our faith walk. It is our only true source of faith, therefore we don't treat it lightly, dilute it or ignore it. Our faith can only come from the word of God. It does not find its origin in the opinions of others. It does not come from prophecy [which is a bonus being an exhorter, an encouragement and a strengthener]. Neither does faith come from past victories.

ROMANS 10:17 NKJV

So then faith comes by hearing, and hearing by the word of God.

QUESTION

When searching out truth in the Bible with your need on your mind, how are you led to read and then pray, knowing your faith depends on the verses you will be looking at?

NOTES

NOTES

11

God is our all-sufficient source and He wants to be involved in every area of our lives. It is not healthy or honouring to have hidden fears or areas of secrecy for there the enemy sets up camp with lies and accusation.

ACTS 17:28 NKJV

For in Him we live and move and have our being.

TASK

Take time to explore the deep thoughts about which you're believing and praying, and see if you are as transparent as you need to be before The Lord. He already knows all there is to know, but sharing yourself with Him in private prayer gives more room for Him to move in you, through you and for you.

NOTES

NOTES

12

We must not forget to keep on mixing faith with the word. The Holy Spirit wants to direct us and the more scripture we read the more the Holy Spirit has to work with. We must keep combining what we have already received with more of the word for faith to grow, just as bread needs to be kneaded and proven more than once for it to rise.

HEBREWS 4:2

For indeed we have had the glad tidings [Gospel of God] proclaimed to us just as truly as they [the Israelites of old did when the good news of deliverance from bondage came to them]; but the message they heard did not benefit them, because it was not mixed with faith (with the leaning of the entire personality on God in absolute trust and confidence in His power, wisdom, and goodness) by those who heard it; neither were they united in faith with the ones [Joshua and Caleb] who heard (did believe).

QUESTION

Think about this scripture and what it is describing from the Old Testament. What was their mistake? How do you want to be different?

NOTES

NOTES

13

The Bible tells us that He who is faithful will do it! He is our provider and He has an answer ready for us even before we ask anything of Him. God is never caught out by our requests, in fact he runs to meet us.

ISAIAH 65:24

And it shall be that before they call I will answer; and while they are yet speaking I will hear.

QUESTION

Do you already have or know of a testimony
of this type of answered prayer that you
can write down here? It will encourage you
today.

NOTES

NOTES

14

People and sometimes even leaders can say that their experience disproves the word of God. How dare they? Even God places His word over His name! We can imagine the angels worshipping as they witness God performing His promises. We must value and use the authority of His word. His word is everlasting and unchanging through the seasons of fashionable teaching that come and go. His word stands and is stronger than any advice given or title another commentator may carry.

PSALM 138:2

I will worship toward Your holy temple and praise Your name for Your loving-kindness and for Your truth and faithfulness; for You have exalted above all else Your name and Your word and You have magnified Your word above all Your name!

EXERCISE

How do you allow others to affect your faith? Do their words align with scripture? Does their stature, title or position intimidate you? Where does God place His name and His word in this verse? Write it here in your own handwriting with the reference in full. Pray over and vocally repeat this truth today.

NOTES

NOTES

15

We value the power of the word in that it divides between what's right and wrong and brings the wisdom of God's heart into any situation.

HEBREWS 4:12

For the Word that God speaks is alive and full of power [making it active, operative, energising, and effective]; it is sharper than any two-edged sword, penetrating to the dividing line of the breath of life (soul) and [the immortal] spirit, and of joints and marrow [of the deepest parts of our nature], exposing and sifting and analysing and judging the very thoughts and purposes of the heart.

TASK

What subtle or obvious differences does the word bring to your expectations today? Can you describe and list them here?

NOTES

NOTES

16

It's comforting, exciting and essential to know that God's word brings direction. We take the time to ask Him to shine His light on our situation and to show us what He has to say about it.

PSALM 119:105

Your word is a lamp to my feet and a light to my path.

CHALLENGE

How would you explain and describe to a nonbeliever that the Bible has helped you in your dilemma? Write your explanation here so that when you share you will be more prepared.

NOTES

NOTES

17

The Bible states that Jesus is the Word and He is the way, the truth and the life. He is the only one to follow, His ways are best and His truth is full and impenetrable.

JOHN 14:6

Jesus said to him, 'I am the way, and the truth, and the life. No one comes to the Father except by (through) Me.

TASK

When you read the word you are having fellowship with Jesus and spending time with Him. What has He shown you of Himself today in His word?

NOTES

NOTES

18

Scripture tells us that the Word was before all things. The Word has an eternal perspective that cuts through time and space. It is not geographically, historically or culturally challenged.

JOHN 1:1+14

IN THE beginning [before all time] was the Word (Christ), and the Word was with God, and the Word was God Himself. And the Word (Christ) became flesh (human, incarnate) and tabernacled (fixed His tent of flesh, lived awhile) among us; and we [actually] saw His glory (His honour, His majesty), such glory as an only begotten son receives from his father, full of grace (favour, loving-kindness) and truth.

QUESTION

Where else in the bible do you find a scripture that speaks of how constant and unchanging Jesus is? Write it here with the reference for your encouragement and pray over it throughout the day.

NOTES

NOTES

19

Everything is in constant fluctuation and it is popular to update and reinvent things these days. It is not so with the Bible. The word of God, although consistently fresh, lasts forever and is our enduring plumb line alongside which we can measure anything.

1 PETER 1:25 NKJV

But the word of the Lord endures forever.

TASK

Into how many areas of your life are you grateful for bringing the faithful and reliable word of God? What have you realistically and practically submitted to His wisdom and viewpoint?

NOTES

NOTES

20

Medical, financial and social opinions continue to be updated and changed. These things sometimes need to be looked at, but God is our final authority. The Lord is our constant companion whose power never weakens, differs or runs out.

HEBREWS 13:8

Jesus Christ (the Messiah) is (always) the same, yesterday, today, (yes) and forever (to the ages).

QUESTION

How do you handle the opinion of the day
(without becoming rude towards others)
while protecting your belief and faith walk in
this ever-changing world?

NOTES

NOTES

21

Whatever our current circumstance and our past failures or successes, we have the opportunity—and most likely the great need—to search out a fresh and relevant word for this moment in time. There is always a scripture that can help for every situation.

2 TIMOTHY 3:16-17

Every Scripture is God-breathed (given by His inspiration) and profitable for instruction, for reproof and conviction of sin, for correction of error and discipline in obedience, [and] for training in righteousness (in holy living, in conformity to God's will in thought, purpose, and action), So that the man of God may be complete and proficient, well fitted and thoroughly equipped for every good work.

TASK

Write here about the other tools and resources you could use to help you in your search for accurate, relevant and useful scriptures. Think carefully, broadly and outside the box. Check out the root of the source, not just the fruit.

NOTES

NOTES

22

We read at the very beginning of the study that God exists and that He is the rewarder of those who earnestly and diligently seek Him [out]. God is kind, diligent and faithful in that He watches over His word to perform it.

JEREMIAH 1:12

Then said the Lord to me, You have seen well, for I am alert and active, watching over My word to perform it.

EXERCISE

Take time to search out and write some other descriptive words and scriptures (with the relevant chapter and verse information) that magnify the true, kind and good nature of God.

NOTES

NOTES

23

Others may try to take authority over us and our circumstances. Their expert opinion and advice may sound very authoritative and overwhelming. Should we always listen and follow through with their instruction?

ISAIAH 45:22-23

Look to me and be saved, all the ends of the earth! For I am God, and there is no other. I have sworn by Myself, the word is gone out of my mouth in righteousness and shall not return, that unto Me every knee shall bow, every tongue shall swear (allegiance).

QUESTION

Which people have tried to steer you away
from believing what God has said. How did
you respond to their opinion?

NOTES

NOTES

24

Faith has to be for a specific thing and it has to be active right now for it to be of any use at all. It is not to be confused with vague, emotional and often deferred hope. Hope says, 'one day', faith says 'today'.

HEBREWS 11:1
NOW FAITH is the assurance (the confirmation, the title deed) of the things [we] hope for, being the proof of things [we] do not see and the conviction of their reality [faith perceiving as real fact what is not revealed to the senses].

QUESTION

Write here what you began by hoping for
and what you now have faith for. What
clinched it for you and turned it into
certainty?

NOTES

NOTES

25

On our faith journey there is always a starting point and we must make an initial decision, even if it's to stand still! Maybe we cannot or dare not think of the full picture or the biggest challenge. If that's the case we begin with an easier more accessible goal. We pray, believing for the first stage in the journey, starting with something we can believe for, then we build on things from there.

MARK 11:24

For this reason I am telling you, whatever you ask for in prayer, believe (trust and be confident) that it is granted to you, and you will [get it].

TASK

Can you see and share how your journey began and how you have seen your faith grow? It may be in the realm of finance, healing or some other area of life.

NOTES

NOTES

26

We learn to lean on our inner man and the thoughts that flow from our heart. We do not trust in, or rely on, our natural view of things as perceived through what we can physically see. We learn to navigate, make judgements and decisions by our spirit and not through our natural perspective.

2 CORINTHIANS 5:7 NKJV

For we walk by faith, not by sight.

QUESTION

When growing this skill, you will find that others don't understand or agree. How will you handle discouragement or the ridicule and scrutiny of others who don't see things your way?

NOTES

NOTES

27

Through faith in Christ, we see what grace has done for us. Grace and faith work together. Ephesians 2:8 tells us 'We are saved by grace and this not of ourselves.' We mature when we allow these attributes to function and work alongside each other.

ROMANS 5:2

Through Him also we have [our] access (entrance, introduction) by faith into this grace (state of God's favour) in which we [firmly and safely] stand.

TASK

Write about what the grace of God means
to you and what it has done for you.
Spend some time in prayer to remember,
acknowledge and thank The Lord for His
immeasurable gift of grace toward you.

NOTES

NOTES

28

Our relationships matter more to our faith journey than most of all the other influences in our life. We will become like the people we spend our time with! Agreement isn't just a lack of argument, it is a joining, union and bond that creates tremendous resolve and strength in the face of tests and trial. It is a good thing to agree with someone concerning our faith journey and to see it work!

MATTHEW 18:19

Again I tell you, if two of you on earth agree (harmonise together, make a symphony together) about whatever [anything and everything] they may ask, it will come to pass and be done for them by My Father in heaven.

CHALLENGE

You see how disharmony won't work here! So, who you share your heart with concerning your faith issue is very important. Think about it! Does their response take you on into believing God more and does it make you want to search out the intentions of His heart from the word? Or does their response unnerve you and try to slow you down by making you comfortable with how far you've come already, knowing the road ahead could be troublesome and tough?

How will you reach your desired goal now if they're negative and you allow them to influence your decisions? Who will you lean on?

Here also is a word of caution:

Negativity is obvious, but when it's clothed in love, empathy and understanding it can be a silent killer. Sometimes you even have to distance your faith walk from people that love you too much. However, please don't be disrespectful or argumentative as this is ungodly and it's really not putting your emotional energy to good use!

Be discerning. Be polite. Be decisive. You don't have to explain your decisions, and you are the one who will live with the consequences.

NOTES

NOTES

29

When 'unity' is called on the stage of a theatrical show everyone finds their role and gets into their position. Anything or anyone that is not needed right there and then on the stage, (eg, make-up artist or costume designer) has to be moved off set. Unity is awesome. It's peaceful, clear and empowering. Everything is freed up to function without hindrance. It is the moment when obstacles, distractions and confusion are removed and clarity comes. This is just what we need when there's a battle raging and victory is in sight!

God will bless those in unity.

PSALM 133:1+3 NKJV

Behold, how good and how pleasant it is for brethren to dwell together in unity... For there the Lord commanded the blessing life forevermore.

TASK

Are there hindrances, interfering parties or confusing influences playing an unauthorised role in your battle right now? Take the time to call out 'unity' and prune back the noise of newspapers, books, opinions, and voices, TV programmes, songs, films or memories that may be muddling your view and prayer life.

NOTES

NOTES

30

Having someone who loves us enough to not let us give up is crucial, and they won't if they have seen the goal as we have and caught it with a passion. When they believe the promises they are far more likely to support us and encourage us on to success. It's crucial for us to be in agreement with people of like heart as they will help us to carry on.

2 CORINTHIANS 1:20

For as many as are the promises of God, they all find their Yes [answer] in Him [Christ]. For this reason we also utter the Amen (so be it) to God through Him [in His Person and by His agency] to the glory of God.

TASK

Do you know how important it is to go to God for your word before you lean on anyone else for encouragement? Do you see that they also need to be people who, with you, deeply value and work with the word of God? Pray about this for a while today.

NOTES

NOTES

31

Agreeing with the promises of God is the best foundation for our lives if we are to reap any fruits and rewards of faith. God has been so kind as to write down His heart and intention for us so that we can avoid the pitfalls of forgetting, confusing or changing it in any way.

1 PETER 2:9

But you are a chosen race, a royal priesthood, a dedicated nation, [God's] own purchased, special people, that you may set forth the wonderful deeds and display the virtues and perfections of Him Who called you out of darkness into His marvellous light.

TASK

Research the meanings of the words royal, dedicated, purchased and special. Pray over each one with gratitude and truly express your acknowledgement and thanks to God for the power they carry for you personally.

NOTES

NOTES

32

Faith works with patience. In the story found in the book of Daniel and chapter 10 we see an angel was commissioned on the first day that prayer went up, but it took 21 days to bring the answer through to Daniel. If he had given up or walked away, conceived his own plan and strategy, or simply changed his request he would have lost the victory.

DANIEL 10:10-13

And [the angel] said to me, O Daniel, you greatly beloved man, understand the words that I speak to you and stand upright, for to you I am now sent. And while he was saying this word to me, I stood up trembling.

Then he said to me, Fear not, Daniel, for from the first day that you set your mind and heart to understand and to humble yourself before your God, your words were heard, and I have come as a consequence of [and in response to] your words.

But the prince of the kingdom of Persia withstood me for twenty- one days. Then Michael, one of the chief [of the celestial] princes, came to help me, for I remained there with the kings of Persia.

TASK

Reaffirm and confess out loud today that you will stay the course and see this through knowing confidently that you were heard in heaven the very first time you called on God in prayer.

NOTES

NOTES

33

Here God strongly confirms we are to endure patiently and be mindful of His timing. He tells us to protect our confidence and shows us how to move forward while obtaining the rewards.

HEBREWS 10:35-39

Do not, therefore, fling away your fearless confidence, for it carries a great and glorious compensation of reward.

For you have need of steadfast patience and endurance, so that you may perform and fully accomplish the will of God, and thus receive and carry away (and enjoy to the full) what is promised.

For still a little while (a very little while) and the Coming One will come and He will not delay.

But the just shall live by faith (My righteous servant shall live by his conviction respecting man's relationship to God and divine things, and holy fervour born of faith and conjoined with it); and if he draws back and shrinks in fear, My soul has not delight or pleasure in him.

But our way is not that of those who draw back to eternal misery (perdition) and are utterly destroyed but we are of those who believe (who cleave to and trust in and rely on God through Jesus Christ, the Messiah) and by faith preserve the soul.

TASK

Read this scripture three times and write out the specific parts of it that have gripped you today. What has impacted you? How has it challenged or changed your thinking and what part of your behaviour is going to be affected?

NOTES

NOTES

34

We must keep believing and choose not to be discouraged. It's not a sin to feel down about our challenge, but it will become a sin if we stay down. Remember that delay is not defeat!!

HEBREWS 10:37-38 NKJV

For yet a little while and He who is coming will come and will not tarry. Now the just shall live by faith, but if anyone draws back, My soul has no pleasure in him.

STUDY

Go and search the scriptures to remind
yourself of what Jesus purchased for you
with His blood, and what He defeated when
He rose again. Take some time to write your
findings here!

NOTES

NOTES

35

Our approach to God as we come to Him in prayer matters more than we can imagine. Always coming thankfully into a prayer conversation opens up the pathway for faith to flow. Speaking and singing out loud to Him with thanks and trust is a powerful biblical (and priceless) habit to develop.

PSALM 100:4

Enter into His gates with thanksgiving and a thank offering and into His courts with praise! Be thankful and say so to Him, bless and affectionately praise His name!

TASK

What can you thank Him for today and at this point in your journey? Remember those previously answered prayers; name the people He has already sent to help you, and the breakthroughs you've experienced up to now.

NOTES

NOTES

36

Staying focused on truth and being secure in our grounded and researched knowledge will prevent us from taking too many detours or having too many 'off' days. The word of God is completely trustworthy and proven truth, and it is the best antidote to fear, worry or confusion. People perish through a lack of knowledge and not always because of a weak constitution or the discouragement of the enemy.

PSALM 119:113

I hate the thoughts of undecided [in religion], double-minded people, but Your law do I love.

TASK

Gird your mind and load yourself up with biblical ammunition!! Get your feet on solid ground. Write out three promises here that correspond with your immediate position and pray over them with thankfulness that God provided for you again!!

NOTES

NOTES

37

Perseverance is essential. We see here that Abraham persevered and therefore he did not falter or waver. Pressures can make it appear easier for us to try and fix things ourselves rather than wait on God. It sometimes looks like it would be easier to give up, but we must not.

ROMANS 4:20

And [Abraham] did not waver at the promise of God through unbelief, but was strengthened in faith, giving glory to God.

STUDY

When you look in the Bible and at his story
was Abraham born perfect and pleasing
to God? What, in his case, was reckoned
to him as righteousness? Take some time
today to go back into the Old Testament to
search this out.

NOTES

NOTES

38

We cannot be of two minds going first this way and then that, believing and praying for one thing and then changing it to another. It will take commitment as the days go by and as challenges arise. We must stay on track and be determined to push through tough days. It's always good to ask God for encouragement and for Him to confirm that we are on time and in tune with His plan. He will talk to us if we stay attentive and open.

JAMES 1:7-8

For truly, let not such a person imagine that he will receive anything [he asks for] from the Lord, [For being as he is] a man of two minds (hesitating, dubious, irresolute), [he is] unstable and unreliable and uncertain about everything [he thinks, feels, decides].

CHALLENGE

List two or three of the main things that you're believing for and praying through. Make them clear enough, so that if your prayer partner asked you about them you could explain your position and describe them immediately.

NOTES

NOTES

39

Endurance is essential when building and nurturing a life of faith. Sometimes decisions are difficult to make and we may have to stand in an uncomfortable place, but settling upon the right choices is very much worth it.

HEBREWS 11:24-25

[Aroused] by faith Moses, when he had grown to maturity and become great, refused to be called the son of Pharaoh's daughter. Because he preferred to share the oppression [suffer the hardships] and bear the shame of the people of God rather than to have the fleeting enjoyment of a sinful life.

QUESTION

A while ago I asked you to trim back the influences that were crowding into your faith journey and blocking out the voice of God. Can you name three or four things that were hampering your thought life that you have given up, stopped reading, watching or listening to since then?

NOTES

NOTES

40

Father God enjoys our company. He wants to share the journey with us and to be involved in every new stage of our faith's development. By allowing Him the blessing of being a hands-on dad in every season, we prove that we are trusting Him by letting Him know what's inside our head and heart.

PSALM 37:3-5

Trust (lean on, rely on, be confident) in the Lord, and do good: so shall you dwell in the land and feed surely on His faithfulness, and truly you shall be fed. Delight yourself also in the Lord, and He will give you the desires and secret petitions of your heart. Commit your way to the Lord [roll and repose each care of your load on Him]; trust, (lean on, rely on, and be confident) also in Him, and He will bring it to pass.

TASK

Many people grew up with distant, distracted or disabled father figures. Work took them away or they were overwhelmed by their own issues and challenges. Our God is different, He is willing and He is able. List six things here that you would like to experience within your relationship with Him and see what He will do for you.

NOTES

NOTES

41

Father God doesn't change, even when everything or everyone else does. When Jesus was on the cross and at the third hour, it went dark. God had turned away from Jesus! I believe He did that then, so that He doesn't have to turn away from us today.

JAMES 1:17

Every good gift and every perfect (free, large, full) gift is from above; it comes down from the Father of all [that gives] light, in [the shining of] Whom there can be no variation [rising or setting] or shadow cast by His turning [as in an eclipse].

TASK

Sing a new song (make a new one up)
of thanks for God's faithful love and
commitment toward you. He promised
never to leave you, only to love you, and be
with you forever.

NOTES

NOTES

42

We can always rely on the word of God to give us confidence as it portrays and describes His heart, His attributes and His intentions in detail. We can be sure of His character in every circumstance and season of our lives.

JOSHUA 1:9

Have not I commanded you? Be strong, vigorous, and very courageous. Be not afraid, neither be dismayed, for the Lord your God is with you wherever you go.

EXERCISE

How has God comforted you by showing
His faithful commitment to you in recent
days? Can you write a simple and clear
testimony here?

NOTES

NOTES

43

Taking care of the words we speak is essential and vital if we're to reap good fruit from them. It's better to say nothing than repeat what we've heard if ever we're overcome with concern at any point. Even so, we can always repent of bad and destructive words that we've spoken and we thank God for His forgiveness.

PROVERBS 18:21
Death and life are in the power of the tongue, and they who indulge in it shall eat the fruit of it (for death or life).

QUESTION

Do the words seen and heard in your world
of TV programmes, friendship and literature
help or hinder your thoughts and spoken
language? What should you take an axe to
and cut out of your life?

NOTES

NOTES

44

It must be emphasised again that during our fight of faith we must be careful with the words we think and then probably go on to speak. Talk is not cheap and it can cost us everything if we don't bridle it well. It takes discipline to keep our speech consistently helpful and faith filled.

HEBREWS 10:23
So let us seize and hold fast and retain without wavering the hope we cherish and confess and our acknowledgement of it, for He Who promised is reliable (sure) and faithful to His word.

QUESTION

Where are you when you talk to yourself? In the shower or the car, at the sink or the bus stop? Do your words align with and agree with the prayers you so passionately pray? Or, do they dribble out like runaway trains that stray from the tracks you carefully put down? Begin to monitor your self-talk as if your life depended on it. It probably does!

NOTES

NOTES

45

Our self-talk is a very strong force in our life as we see from the verse below. We must take great care and monitor the small, unnoticed phrases that we verbalise so often.

JAMES 1:26

If anyone thinks himself to be religious (piously observant of the external duties of his faith) and does not bridle his tongue but deludes his own heart, this person's religious service is worthless (futile, barren).

TASK

Take time today to write the phrases you've
picked up, learned and often repeat that
you actually, don't agree with, don't like
or don't need in your life. Choose to stop
saying phrases such as, 'It does my head in',
'I'm torn', 'It makes me sick.'

NOTES

NOTES

46

We see the tongue can be full of poison and therefore has the potential to create havoc. God used His words positively and created the world. We are made in His image and can create our environment with our words.

JAMES 3:5+8

Even so the tongue is a little member, and it can boast of great things. See how much wood or how great a forest a tiny spark can set ablaze! But the human tongue can be tamed by no man. It is a restless (undisciplined, irreconcilable) evil, full of deadly poison.

QUESTION

How do you need to change your general vocabulary and language to create the world and life that you want to live in?

NOTES

NOTES

47

The Holy Spirit will work on the word that we put into our mind and memory. Therefore, reading more will give Him more to work with. Taking a few verses at a time and searching for something specific will give our reading time more purpose and meaning. The Bible will never be dull after this!

ROMANS 10:8 NKJV

But what does it say? "The word is near you, in your mouth and in your heart" (that is, the word of faith which we preach)...

TASK

Think of four key topics such as health, peace or finance that affect your fight of faith and search for specific scriptures that you can think on and learn from. Aim to find out the context of the verses so that you keep things in perspective.

NOTES

NOTES

48

The Holy Spirit has been sent to us to help in every area of our lives. He will not be offended if we involve Him in the difficult or messy challenges, in fact He is grieved when we forget to ask for help or choose to exclude Him.

ROMANS 8:26 NKJV
Likewise the Spirit also helps in our weaknesses. For we do not know what we should pray for as we ought, but the Spirit Himself makes intercession for us with groanings which cannot be uttered.

TASK

Take time to pray through your recent
situation and ask the Holy Spirit to
get involved in every corner of your
complicated story. Hold nothing back
because He knows you and is for you!

NOTES

NOTES

49

Intelligent, intuitive and insightful faith is a gift from God, and we lean into Him for this. Chaos, frustration and fear are not a part of His plan, in fact He wants us to be ahead of the game, in control and in the driving seat.

In my book '*Is God There? You Bet!*'

I describe in detail how God intervened and specifically directed us through many difficult times and serious challenges. As a result our stolen property was restored, our children's lives were saved in the face of grave danger and God gave us the upper hand in property deals. We are so grateful that He loves, leads, and speaks to us, and we give Him all the glory!

DEUTERONOMY 28:13

·And the Lord shall make you the head, and not the tail; and you shall be above only, and you shall not be beneath...

QUESTION

What has the Holy Spirit warned you to do
or not to do in order to put you in the lead
position concerning your circumstances?
Write your testimony here or spend time
praying that this can become part of your
story as you reach for your victory.

NOTES

NOTES

50

The Holy Spirit is released or hindered
by the words we speak and the manner
in which we say them. Faith filled words
uttered from a thankful and trusting heart
are what move the Holy Spirit to action.

1 PETER 3:9-10

Never return evil for evil or insult for insult
(scolding, tongue-lashing, berating), but
on the contrary blessing [praying for their
welfare, happiness, and protection, and truly
pitying and loving them]. For know that
to this you have been called, that you may
yourselves inherit a blessing [from God—that
you may obtain a blessing as heirs, bringing
welfare and happiness and protection]. For
let him who wants to enjoy life and see good
days [good—whether apparent or not] keep
his tongue free from evil and his lips from
guile (treachery, deceit).

TASK

How can you begin to change the way you live to bring your words and actions into line?

a) Replace a lie with the truth?

b) Stop yourself confessing something that you don't want to happen?

c) Feed on faith books instead of magazines or recent media coverage?

NOTES

NOTES

51

To live in love is essential on our journey of faith! If we think it's only about success and our big breakthrough then we're missing the point. To help others find the love and provision of God is a very important part of the life He has planned for us.

JAMES 2:15-16

If a brother or sister is poorly clad and lacks food for each day, And one of you says to him, Good-bye! Keep [yourself] warm and well fed, without giving him the necessities for the body, what good does that do?

TASK

Can you take your eyes off your own needs and help another person less fortunate than yourself? Prepare to bless someone else today and write down not only your intended actions but also your specific desire for their blessing. Decide to build this into your daily lifestyle.

NOTES

NOTES

52

Love should be the key and motivating factor when it comes to fruit- bearing faith. Driven, selfish or cold ambitious faith will amount to nothing. May we let love play its part and do its work.

GALATIANS 5:6

For [if we are] in Christ Jesus, neither circumcision nor uncircumcision counts for anything, but only faith activated and energised and expressed and working through love.

QUESTION

How has love inspired and shaped your faith journey? I'm hoping your love for The Lord, the lost and your saved family and friends will have grown over these recent weeks. Can you write down your thoughts and share the changes you've experienced?

NOTES

NOTES

53

To be a blessing and to not just want to be blessed is a very powerful way to live. To look out for the needs of others in the midst of trial can be a life-giving, even life- saving experience. See the double blessing that comes from a life lived like this!

PSALM 41:1-3

BLESSED (HAPPY, fortunate, to be envied) is he who considers the weak and the poor; the Lord will deliver him in the time of evil and trouble. The Lord will protect him and keep him alive; he shall be called blessed in the land; and You will not deliver him to the will of his enemies. The Lord will sustain, refresh, and strengthen him on his bed of languishing; all his bed You [O Lord] will turn, change, and transform in his illness.

TASK

The Bible says the poor will be with us
always and their needs will continually be a
part of life. You are blessed every day while
you have clothes on your back and food
in your stomach. Could you be a continual
support to someone less fortunate than
yourself and release a double blessing?

NOTES

NOTES

54

The love of God overflows and gives us concern for the welfare of others. This is agape love and it is the kind of love that releases faith. Faith is not a spiritual power to be used to make us look good but it will produce results when we use it to meet the needs of others.

1 CORINTHIANS 13:2

And if I have prophetic powers (the gift of interpreting the divine will and purpose), and understand all the secret truths and mysteries and possess all knowledge, and if I have [sufficient] faith so that I can remove mountains, but have not love (God's love in me) I am nothing (a useless nobody).

QUESTION

What kind of love do you need to develop in order to outwork the concern you have for others? Your faith will grow when it's released through love and on the behalf of those less fortunate than yourself.

NOTES

NOTES

55

Faith working through love is never aggressive, or ambitious in a selfish way. It causes us to long for the health, prosperity and success of another. We find ourselves wanting the provision and power so that we can bless others and heal them.

ACTS 10:38

How God anointed and consecrated Jesus of Nazareth with the [Holy] Spirit and with strength and ability and power; how He went about doing good and, in particular, curing all who were harassed and oppressed by [the power of] the devil, for God was with Him.

QUESTION

Are you willing for God to increase your faith so that people can come to you for provision, help and miracles? Would you support and partner with a ministry already established in this kind of work?

NOTES

NOTES

56

Faith working through love is more productive than emotion! It actually moves us from compassion to action! There is enough need in our towns for people everywhere to bear fruit through anointed giving. Time, money, love and attention are all gifts that can be donated to the poor and it's good to give to others and take care of them.

JAMES 2:17

So also faith, if it does not have works (deeds and actions of obedience to back it up), by itself is destitute of power (inoperative, dead).

TASK

Do you know of local agencies that need help where you could volunteer and support for a few hours a week? Many find it convenient or glamorous to serve abroad when true love begins at home.

NOTES

NOTES

57

The act of giving releases a powerful and positive force in our lives. Guilt is also powerful but in a negative way as it is disruptive and causes faith to be aborted. It is destructive in the way it affects and hinders prayer. To have a clear conscience is essential as we reach for answers. See below how God has faithfully given a loving promise here in Hebrews.

HEBREWS 10:22

Let us all come forward and draw near with true (honest and sincere) hearts in unqualified assurance and absolute conviction engendered by faith (by that leaning of the entire human personality on God in absolute trust and confidence in His power, wisdom, and goodness), having our hearts sprinkled and purified form a guilty (evil) conscience and our bodies cleansed with pure water.

TASK

Take time today to fellowship with your heavenly Father and allow His love to deal with any regrets, mistakes or wrongdoings that you need to be cleansed of. He knows you and wants you to be free in Jesus name.

NOTES

NOTES

58

The word of God has to be our final authority on every issue. Everything else will shift and change depending on our mood and circumstances. Make His word your plumb line for every decision and request.

JOHN 15:7

If you live in Me [abide vitally united to Me] and My words remain in you and continue to live in your hearts, ask whatever you will, and it shall be done for you.

TASK

Write down three scriptures that have shaped the development of your faith in these recent weeks. Think deeply about how your views and perspectives have changed and thank God for this.

NOTES

NOTES

59

The word of God can overrule our original and inherited mindset because when Christ dwells in us by His Spirit our mind is constantly renewed.

1 CORINTHIANS 2:16

For who has known or understood the mind (the counsels and purposes) of the Lord so as to guide and instruct Him and give Him knowledge? But we have the mind of Christ (the Messiah) and do hold the thoughts (feelings and purposes) of His heart.

QUESTION

How has your mind been changed when considering the promises you have discovered? How did you used to think? What does your overall mindset and approach look like now?

NOTES

NOTES

60

Over the next few pages we will see some of the benefits of exercising our faith and the good things that are released into our lives. We must acknowledge that this has been a spiritual experience and not merely a mental challenge.

2 CORINTHIANS 10:3-4

For though we walk (live) in the flesh, we are not carrying on our warfare according to the flesh and using mere human weapons. For the weapons of our warfare are not physical (weapons of flesh and blood), but they are mighty before God for the overthrow and destruction of strongholds...

QUESTION

What does the verse above say your weapons are, and what is to be the result of their application in your life?

NOTES

NOTES

61

Faith will produce the blessing of eternal salvation. Through faith we accept Jesus Christ as Saviour and Lord and we are saved from sin, its consequential death and eternity without Him.

1 PETER 1:9

[At the same time] you receive the result (outcome, consummation) of your faith, the salvation of your souls.

QUESTION

Do you know who prayed for you so that you heard the gospel and were saved? How did your story unfold? How fervently are you praying for your friend or family member to become a believer?

NOTES

NOTES

62

Faith will produce the blessing of righteousness!

Forgiveness was given in the Old Testament through repeated animal sacrifice. Jesus was made our scapegoat once and for all and we are made righteous! Now through faith we can live and be totally acceptable before a Holy God.

ROMANS 1:16-17 NASB

For I am not ashamed of the gospel, for it is the power of God for salvation to everyone who believes, to the Jew first and also to the Greek. For in it the righteousness of God is revealed from faith to faith; as it is written, "But the righteous man shall live by faith."

TASK

The gospel is an amazing message. How has your understanding been changed? Where have you overcome fear, doubt and dead works? Could you practise and learn to share your story of salvation in less than five minutes?

1 PETER 3:15

But in your hearts set Christ apart as holy [and acknowledge Him] as Lord. Always be ready to give a logical defence to anyone who asks you to account for the hope that is in you, but do it courteously and respectfully.

NOTES

NOTES

63

Faith will produce the blessing of eternal life. To live with purpose and in peace is a luxury for many and out of reach for most. To live in this state eternally is a precious and gracious gift of God.

1 JOHN 2:25

And this is what He Himself has promised us—the life, the eternal [life].

REQUEST

Even in your challenge remember that if God never answered another prayer of yours He has already done more than enough for you if you have eternal life. Please always remember to pray for and share your faith with those who don't know and live in the One you've come to know and love.

NOTES

NOTES

64

Faith will produce the blessing of peace. There is nothing we can do to make God love us more. He is love and there is nothing we can do to make Him love us less! Now we've been forever reconciled with our maker.

ROMANS 5:1-2

Therefore, since we are justified by faith, we have peace with God through our Lord Jesus Christ. Through Him we have obtained access to this grace in which we stand, and we rejoice in our hope of sharing the glory of God.

TASK

Please find and write two more scriptures that promise peace for yourself and those you are praying for. Write them here in full with the chapter and verse references.

NOTES

NOTES

65

Faith will produce the blessing of full citizenship within the Kingdom of heaven. To belong is one of the most basic human needs. Here we are welcomed and received into an unshakeable community!

HEBREWS 12:28

Let us therefore, receiving a kingdom that is firm and stable and cannot be shaken, offer to God pleasing service and acceptable worship, with modesty and pious care and godly fear and awe...

TASK

Take time to imagine and delight in the reassurance that this sense of belonging has brought to your life. You are accepted, received and included in something of eternal worth.

NOTES

NOTES

66

Faith will produce the blessing of eternal protection. To be protected for a day would be the answer to many a person's prayer these days.

Within this Kingdom and under the care of The King of Kings you are protected for eternity and this is outrageously good!

1 PETER 1:3-6

Praised (honoured, blessed) be the God and Father of our Lord Jesus Christ (the Messiah)! By His boundless mercy we have been born again to an ever-living hope through the resurrection of Jesus Christ from the dead, [Born anew] into an inheritance which is beyond the reach of change and decay [imperishable], unsullied and unfading, reserved in heaven for you, Who are being guarded (garrisoned) by God's power through [your] faith [till you fully inherit that final] salvation that is ready to be revealed

[for you] in the last time. [You should] be
exceedingly glad on this account, though now
for a little while you may be distressed by
trials and suffer temptations...

TASK

What kind of protection are you particularly
grateful for? Write out your thoughts and
pray specifically and thankfully for each
experience.

NOTES

NOTES

67

Faith will reveal the blessing of the faithfulness of God! Sometimes we have confidence in our own ability to have faith rather than leaning on God. Our faith should be in God and His word. God will take us as far as we are willing to go and it is faith in Him that we should be focussing on. We must never give up or lose heart because He doesn't grow tired or weary of us.

PHILIPPIANS 1:6

And I am convinced and sure of this very thing that He Who began a good work in you will continue until the day of Jesus Christ (right up to the time of His return) developing (that good work) and perfecting and bringing it to full completion in you.

EXERCISE

Resolve today to continue on in your faith journey. Study to develop your understanding and build your knowledge on what the word says. Never give up when God is preparing you for the next phase. Never put in a full stop where He would place a comma. Move forward every day!!

NOTES

NOTES

68

When we realise The Lord wants us to be mature and to grow in all areas of our faith we will shake off rejection, fear and doubt! He totally believes in who we are and especially in who we were always meant to become.

JOHN 14:12

I assure you, most solemnly I tell you, if anyone steadfastly believes in Me, he will himself be able to do the things that I do; and he will do even greater things than these, because I go to the Father.

TASK

Take time today to dream and imagine about who He has made you to be. Rejoice in His plan and unfailing love for you today!!

NOTES

NOTES

69

God planned that we would bear fruit and fruit that lasts. He planned that all of our lives would influence and bring blessing to others. We see here that the coaching and training up of other people reaps its own rewards.

ISAIAH 54:17

But no weapon that is formed against you shall prosper, and every tongue that shall rise against you in judgment you shall show to be in the wrong. This [peace, righteousness, security, triumph over opposition] is the heritage of the servants of the Lord [those in whom the ideal Servant of the Lord is reproduced]; this is the righteousness or the vindication which they obtain from Me [this is that which I impart to them as their justification], says the Lord.

THOUGHT

I love to share this verse in my class at Destiny College! To see the potential in other people is a great joy to me! Be mindful and give thought to becoming trained and the training up of others, as here God shows Himself especially strong. Where can you receive more training or get involved in the training up of other people? Did you ever consider Destiny College for yourself or to sponsor a friend for a course of study?

NOTES

NOTES

70

God has designed us for great exploits and success. We are not to settle for anything less than His word has promised. Sickness, lack, broken or frustrated potential are not a part of his plan.

EPHESIANS 3:20

Now to Him Who, by (in consequence of) the [action of His] power that is at work within us, is able to [carry out His purpose and] do superabundantly, far over and above all that we [dare] ask or think [infinitely beyond our highest prayers, desires, thoughts, hopes, or dreams]...

STUDY

Continuing to seek out the word, to build positive relationships and outwork your faith will bring rewards. Being planted into a great local church is healthy for you as isolation is never God's design.

NOTES

NOTES

71

Staying under a problem or concern is never God's will for us. In our faith journey there are challenges but how we respond is critical so that we rise above and see good things.

2 SAMUEL 22:33 NKJV

God is my strength and power,
And He makes my way perfect.

STUDY

Take the time to seek out the meaning of the words - strength, power and perfect - in this scripture. Note what God wants you to focus on and change your expectations.

NOTES

NOTES

72

The problems of life and the enemy would want us to be defeated and beaten down. God has a different plan and vision for every believer.

1 CHRONICLES 29:11 AMPC

Yours, O Lord, is the greatness and the power and the glory and the victory and the majesty, for all that is in the heavens and the earth is yours

TASK

Thank the Lord because His greatness on your life means that - His mighty acts, majesty and advancement will all take you forward. Praise Him when you see that His victory (activity and involvement) brings splendour, confidence and strength to your world.

NOTES

NOTES

73

For every problem there's a promise. In the word of God we find there is permission to be positive. Your need should drive you to your knees but with an expectation of answered prayer.

PSALM 34:4 AMPC

I sought (inquired of) the Lord and required Him [of necessity and on the authority of His Word], and He heard me, and delivered me from all my fears.

STUDY

List three of your daily needs that require an answer and search in the concordance of your bible to see what the Lord has to say. What options and remedies does God's word offer you today?

NOTES

NOTES

74

When following Jesus' teachings we're urged to live by the leading of His Spirit. The Holy Spirit is our friend, power house and strengthener.

1 THESSALONIANS 5:17-19 NASB
Pray without ceasing; in everything give thanks; for this is God's will for you in Christ Jesus. Do not quench the Spirit.

TASK

Recently I found myself trying to think why God would ask me to do something. I soon realised it is not my question to ask. Can you think of a moment when you declined or delayed your response to God and the lesson you learned?

NOTES

NOTES

75

Love must motivate. To love is to lift up community. Our energy can be spent on many things but it reaps better rewards when showing true kindness and love to someone.

2 CORINTHIANS 5:14 AKJV

For the love of Christ constraineth us.

TASK

Ask yourself why do you want to build your faith and how do you want to serve God and your community? If it is because of love you will find that your energy is continuous and your endeavours will be held together and in union with Him.

God bless you as you continue to study and find faith to live by. If you would like to find more teachings or send in a prayer request please do contact us at dlr@destiny-church.com. We would be delighted and honoured to offer guidance and support.

NOTES

NOTES

Destiny
Leadership Resources